Sociology
The Scientific Study of Society

Rachael Collinson and Louis Bevoc

Published by
NutriNiche System LLC

Louis Bevoc books...simple explanations of complex subjects

Part One

Introduction

A good way to start a discussion on sociology is by stating that it is quite a diverse subject. In fact, its diversity is often a reason why people are interested in becoming sociologists. Researchers can examine units as small as a family or as large as a worldwide organization. Some studies focus on the impact of divorce on the daily activities of people in a small neighborhood, while others explore the global hierarchy of a multibillion-dollar company. Regardless of the type of work being done, the goal of sociology as a discipline is to understand and explain the behavior of people in society.

Sociology is an important area of study due to its ubiquitous application. It examines people and analyzes their actions, behaviors, and relationships with their environments. It explores social rules, practices, values, beliefs, and norms in an attempt to identify patterns and changes that lead to choices and perceptions. It is about the various cultures that exist, what defines those cultures, and what impact those cultures have on society. Without sociology, there would essentially be no detailed exploration of the relationships between people and society.

Interestingly, interpersonal relationships are usually not the major focus of sociological research. These relationships matter, but they take a back seat to group behavior...which is the major difference between the work done by sociologists and that done by psychologists. Psychologists explore people's minds in order to understand their behavior, while sociologists look at the groups that people are part of in order to understand human behavior. For example, a psychologist might study the emotional responses of a war veteran with PTSD, while a sociologist studies the patterns of behavior that exist in groups of war veterans with PTSD.

There is little doubt that sociology borrows from other areas of study. In addition to psychology, anthropology, and history also lend a little bit of themselves. However, sociology differentiates itself because it has developed into the premier discipline for the scientific study of society.

Some people have questioned the validity of sociology as a science because the participants cannot be studied in the laboratory settings necessary for experimentation and measurement. However, science is based on reasoning and evidence in order to draw valid inferences. Sociologists might not use laboratories for their studies, but they do draw inferences based on scientific methodologies used in a variety of specific fields. They find general answers to questions regarding social processes and human relationships regardless of the location of their research.

Please note that this book does not discuss the history or theories of sociology. Early schools of thought, such as functionalism, and modern developments, such as social stratification, are of great value to the discipline...but discussions on these topics need to come from other sources. Instead, this book focuses on explaining sociology and exemplifying its use in research. In a nutshell, readers will learn about the concepts and applications of this scientific study of society in order to understand its value.

In order to better understand the work that sociologists do, it helps to break them into two types. One type, known as micro-sociology, focuses on small group interactions, while the other type, known as macro-sociology, focuses on large group interactions, social structures, and systems.

Consider research involving the Catholic faith. Micro-sociologists might conduct a study on the social norms of single Catholic females under the age of 21, while macro-sociologists explore the impact of world politics on Catholicism as a whole. Both of these studies use the same organization as the subject matter, but their research involves different levels of that organization.

Not surprisingly, micro-sociologists and macro-sociologists use different research methodologies because those methodologies are best suited for specific types of situations. Both of their approaches to problem-solving have advantages and disadvantages, as shown in the table below.

Type	Advantages	Disadvantages
Micro-sociologist	They have a good idea of what is happening on the ground. They are "in the trenches" and see things close up as they unfold. This allows for a better understanding of human behavior as groups of people interact.	They can get so caught up in their small area of study that they fail to see the whole picture. This can lead to them failing to understand the larger forces that affect changes within the population of the study.
Macro-sociologist	They see large-scale patterns as they develop and can use these patterns	They focus so much on major trends that they fail to see what goes on in

	for a better understanding of human behavior. This provides a realistic analysis of why changes occur within the entire population of the study.	groups of people at the ground level. This can cause them to miss out on the small human interactions that lead to the big picture.

Let's look at a more specific application of micro-sociology and macro-sociology applied to research on politics. The area of study for each type of sociologist is described along with the research methods they employ.

Micro-sociologist

Research question - How has the Democratic Party influenced the behavior of minority students in urban high schools?

Research methodology - This research draws heavily from one-on-one interviews with the minority students to collect first-hand data that can be analyzed for common patterns. Direct observation, also known as ethnography, is also used to find common thinking about the Democratic Party.

Macro-sociologist

Research question - How have politics influenced the behavior of the citizens of the United States?

Research methodology - This research relies on historical data that can be used to gather and analyze statistics that reveal patterns related to specific party alliances. Additionally, interviews are used to make connections between the citizens and their political choices to strengthen the findings of the historical data.

Both sociologists above use qualitative research methods for their work, as is often the case for the social sciences, but qualitative methodology also plays a role in sociological studies. Both methods have their place in research, but quantitative research methods are used to generate measurements of people's behavior, while qualitative research methods are used to find meanings behind people's behavior.

Below are descriptions and examples of quantitative and qualitative methodologies for a better understanding of what they are and why they are used.

Quantitative

Quantitative research is implemented to statistically analyze and measure the way in which people think, feel, and behave. It investigates phenomena. More specifically, it investigates *who, what, when,* and *where* using statistics or mathematics.

Researchers use quantitative methods to collect numerical data and develop theories, models, and hypotheses about the phenomena. Findings can be applied to other situations if they have been replicated in different research.

Advantage

Quantitative research provides precise numerical data that is not influenced by the researcher's personal bias.

Disadvantage

Quantitative research produces findings that are often too generalized for application to specific situations.

Quantitative research can involve experimental controls and the manipulation of variables to obtain numerical data. In short:

- A study with a purpose and significance is proposed and defined (demographically).
- Variables are established.
- Relationships are determined from data collected after manipulating some variables while holding others constant.

An example includes the following:

Lori is a sociologist who owns her own consulting firm. She is hired to determine if race plays a role in groups that support charitable causes. She wants to test this by measuring the relationship between race and commitment to the cause while controlling the type of charity. In this study, race and commitment to the cause both change, but the type of charity is held constant.

Quantitative research can also involve surveys with structured questions used to collect data. In short:

- A study with a purpose and significance is proposed and defined (demographically).
- Variables are established.
- Relationships are determined after collecting data from surveys measuring the variables.

An example includes the following:

Lori believes race impacts group members' commitment to charitable causes. She tests her thinking by measuring the relationship between race and commitment to the cause. She issues surveys (with rating scales) to all members that measure their organizational commitment while asking them to designate their race. The results are then correlated to look for relationships between race and commitment.

Qualitative

Qualitative research is broader than quantitative research. It investigates *why* and *how,* in addition to *who, what, when,* and *where,* using interviews, focus groups, observation, and content analysis.

Researchers use qualitative methods to understand organizational behavior and the reasons for that behavior. Findings can rarely be applied to other situations because they are usually unique to the people in the study.

Advantage

Qualitative research can be applied to complex phenomena.

Disadvantage

Qualitative research results are often influenced by the researcher's personal bias.

Qualitative research can involve surveys with open-ended questions. In short:

- A study with a purpose and significance is proposed and defined (demographically).
- A survey is distributed.
- Findings are determined by looking for patterns in survey responses.

An example includes the following:

Lori believes group members do not trust their group leaders. She wants to determine if members are experiencing trust issues and, if so, the reasons for their distrust. She distributes a survey to all members asking them if they trust the leaders. If their response is no, then they are asked to write about situations they have encountered that caused them to lose trust in leaders. Results are then analyzed for patterns that identify common areas where members lack trust.

Qualitative research can involve ethnography. In short:

- A study with a purpose and significance is proposed and defined (demographically).
- Observations are made.
- Findings are determined by subjectively analyzing the observations.

An example includes the following:

Lori believes members of breast cancer groups form strong interpersonal relationships with each other, and she wants to know if this can be supported. She observes these members for two hours a week over a one-year period, and she notes the conversations they have with each other. She then analyzes those conversations to determine if the members have strong interpersonal bonds with one another.

Now that you understand some of the basic quantitative and qualitative methodologies used during research, let's specify some of the areas that sociologists find interesting to research.

Part Two

Research interests

In one form or another, all human behavior is social. This socializing often takes place in groups that differ in size, direction, goals, and objectives. Sociologists study groups as small as the immediate family to as large as a specific race, social class, gender, or religion. One researcher might study the relationships of a mother with her sons, while another studies the relationship between organized crime and religion. The boundaries of sociological research are virtually endless as long as groups and society are involved.

Sociologists also study social facts. The term "social fact" was coined by sociologist Emile Durkheim in the late 1800s as a factor that limits the choices people have in society. These factors are not physical barriers like mountains or oceans, but they are just as constraining as physical objects because they impose themselves on people. Examples include norms, expectations, beliefs, customs, values, rituals, statuses, roles, and laws.

Social facts are often part of social activities or social institutions, and they dictate what people within can and cannot do. Durkheim explained social facts by imagining a man in a room. This man has the freedom to make choices and move about in the room, but he is limited by physical factors such as doors and windows. He cannot, for example, leave the room through a wall...he must leave through a door or climb out a window. Choices in society are limited in the same way, but the restrictive factors are social rather than physical.

For instance, politically conservative Republicans are expected to be pro-life, while liberal democrats are expected to be pro-choice. Other examples include the norms of saying "good morning" to coworkers when entering the workplace in the morning and shaking hands with new business acquaintances. These types of expectations are not absolute, but people are considered rude or strange if they do not abide by them; thereby resulting in their behavior being limited by social constraints.

In a nutshell, sociologists are interested in the everyday experiences of people and how those experiences are shaped by group or societal interaction. They search for patterns of human behavior within groups of people to identify decision-making processes and reasons for change. Some specific areas of interest for their research include those shown below.

Cults

Cults have long been an area of interest for sociological research due to the general perception people have of them. They are often associated with negative or derogatory connotations that have evolved from (2) past member activities that resulted in harm or wrongdoing and (2) fear of the unknown due to a lack of understanding of member intent. Regardless of the reasoning behind people's thinking about cults, they tend to make good case studies that interest academics and the general public.

Cults are groups that are defined by their often unique philosophies and objectives. Some people believe they are socially deviant in nature, even though that deviance is not always transparent, while others believe they come into being spontaneously when individuals share common thoughts and beliefs. However, regardless of their reason for development, they can range in size from one small group to many large groups, depending on practices, location, norms, and charismatic leadership.

Many cults stem from religious movements. Members within are seeking spiritual guidance that they cannot find in traditional religion. Their common system of beliefs can be very powerful and controversial, sometimes leading to behavior that is not allowed by established laws or unethical in the view of outsiders. This type of behavior makes cults an interesting choice for sociological research.

A simple example of a cult study is as follows:

> A sociologist named Matt is researching wealth patterns of members in faith healing groups. More specifically, he wants to see if there is a relationship between monetary net worth and the belief that prayer and gestures elicit divine intervention for physical healing. Matt's research consists of interviews and direct observation of the cult members, thereby allowing the methodology to be both subjective (interviews and, to a lesser extent, direct observation) and objective (direct observation) in design.

The above study examines the financial status of members of a faith-healing group to see if there are any relationships between their money and their beliefs regarding the power of prayers. The interviews collect the thoughts of the members to discover whether or not they think their beliefs are monetarily driven, while the direct observation functions to remove some of the bias that people might have about their money and their beliefs. When combined, these methods work well to discover patterns that otherwise would not have emerged.

Family

Families are often preferred subject matter for sociological research because they are the most basic social unit found in society. They are a recognized group that has been around since the formation of human societies, and they often influence people more than anything else that they encounter in life.

In recent years, family research has become even more popular due to this social unit becoming more non-traditional in structure. Marriages are not always male/female, single parents raise children, and women have entered the workforce in record numbers. Add to this the fact that an LGBTQ+ lifestyle is more acceptable among children today than it ever was in the past, and it is rather easy to understand that the opportunities for family research have increased.

The change in the structure of families has also created some debate among people regarding the definition of this social unit. Conservative individuals tend to families as being the traditional father, mother, and children, while liberal folk's definition is much broader, regardless of the biological linkages or the number or type of spouses involved. Faced with this dilemma, sociologists often view families as groups where members form emotional connections over long periods of time. This could be through marriage or birth, but it could also evolve as people live together or become close friends.

Regardless of the definition of families, most people believe that they play a critical role in people's lives, which is why they are frequently the focus of sociological research. They shape younger members as those members grow into adults, form bonds with others, and create their own families. Situations can change if families merge to form bigger families, but the impact of this basic social unit remains consistent in terms of the influence it has on members.

Sociological research offers a variety of different perspectives on family relationships. It creates new thoughts and ideas that can be used to examine member differences, find similarities, pinpoint needs, and suggest opportunities for improvement. As a discipline, sociology addresses family problems to understand what is required to bring about the change necessary for finding solutions.

A simple example of a family study is as follows:

> A sociologist named Janet is researching behavior patterns of adolescent male children living in single-female-parent families. She wants to see if the adolescent males' actions can be correlated with the absence of a male parent. Janet's research is based mainly on her direct observation of the adolescent males' behavior, so she can see how they act in different situations, but she also uses one-on-one interviews to look for patterns of thought that exist in regard to living situations.

The above study examines adolescent male behavior in single-female-parent households. The methodologies used are both qualitative, but they differ in the ways that they obtain information. The one-on-one interviews extract individual thoughts of the subjects in order to search for patterns of similar thinking. This is beneficial because all responses are internal and specific to the individual. However, biases that people have about themselves sometimes surface, and those biases can be eliminated using the direct observation method, which functions more objectively.

Religion

Religion is a dichotomy because it functions as a cause of and a resolution for many types of problems in society. It causes people to argue, fight, and even kill each other, while it also resolves issues through forgiveness and the sharing of common beliefs and values. This dual function might appear strange or highly improbable to some individuals, but it makes perfect sense to those who have studied the impact religion has on people and their environments...and it also attracts sociologists looking for interesting research.

Quite simply, sociology is geared toward religious research due to its nature and intent. As noted in the introduction, sociology "explores social rules, practices, values, beliefs, and norms in an attempt to identify patterns and changes that lead to choices and perceptions," and nothing fits these defining principles better than religion.   Add to this the fact that religion is an important aspect of societies all over the globe, and it is relatively easy to see why sociologists are interested in studying it.

Religious organizations create social cohesion (binding of members) and establish social control (common behavior of the members). The comfort experienced by members helps them cope with life's ups and downs and gives them the strength necessary to keep moving forward in life. In many instances, religion provides people with a sense of purpose in this world while preparing them for life in the next.

Another interesting fact about religion is its ability to precipitate change and bring about social reform. It provides the answers and emotional support necessary to establish new thought processes and move in different directions. Martin Luther exemplified this when he took his followers and broke away from Catholicism for protestant reform. He challenged the Catholic belief that good deeds earn eternal life, instead teaching that God's grace is only earned through the acceptance of Jesus Christ as one's savior. This is a very significant change in terms of Christianity, and it would have provided excellent subject matter for sociological research.

Religion is a unique choice for research because it explains the unknown through faith. Members believe something divine exists, even though little or no science-based evidence exists. These beliefs are passed on for generations until they are challenged with some type of reformative process. Martin Luther exemplified this type of challenge on a large scale, but smaller, more subtle changes also take place. For example, some religions have altered the traditional male leadership roles by opening up those roles to women. These changes impact the religions where they take place, but they also affect the communities where those religions are found. This "domino" effect creates even more opportunities for sociologists to conduct their research.

A simple example of a religious study is as follows:

> A sociologist named Marco is researching liberalism and the Methodist church. More specifically, he wants to see if the views of liberal members impact their viewpoints on abortion. To do this, Marco uses survey research to identify liberal members and pro-choice members and then determine if a relationship exists. Numbers from the surveys are compared to see if a correlation can be found.

The above study examines people in a Methodist church to see if their liberalism or conservatism affects their perceptions of abortion. The survey is used to gather the thoughts, beliefs, and opinions of members to see if their political leanings impact their pro-life or pro-choice viewpoints. Unlike most sociological studies, findings are established using only numbers-based quantitative methodology that searches for statistical significance.

Education

It can be said with confidence that education, especially that which is formal, has a major impact on the financial well-being of people. In fact, outside of birthright, education might be the biggest separating factor of wealth in the world today...which is one reason why it is often the focus of research. However, research involving education is not limited to its influence on money. Many researchers, including sociologists, find any type of educational research to be interesting, so they devote a large amount of their time and effort to discovering new things about it.

Sociologists' research involving education is fairly wide open in terms of the specific subject matter, but they often look for behavioral patterns in certain groups of an educated population. For example, they might examine the interpersonal skills of MBA graduates compared to graduates of master's degree programs in the social sciences within the same institution. The findings from this type of study might be beneficial to different groups for specific reasons, as shown below:

Employers

Human resource personnel are often challenged with the task of finding the best job-fit for open positions within their organizations. Job fit refers to how well employees are suited for specific jobs. If it is found that social science graduates have better interpersonal skills, then they might be preferred over MBA graduates when hiring for positions that require a great deal of interaction with others.

Universities and Colleges

These institutions can use the findings to see how well they are preparing graduate students to communicate with others in the real world. They can also use the findings to determine if changes need to be made to their existing degree programs or if new areas of study need to be developed.

Students

Students can use the findings to make more informed decisions about the graduate program that they enroll in. If they know that companies rank interpersonal skills high on their lists of needs, then they can choose the program that best provides them with those skills.

Regardless of the level or type or level of learning, education is derived from schools that function as social institutions where knowledge and skills are obtained. Every country in the world has some type of educational system, but these systems vary in depth of study, subject matter capacity, resource availability, and instructor knowledge based on the wealth of those nations. Yes, as is often the case, the mighty dollar rears its ugly head to take control of the situation.

Sociologists who find education to be an interesting area of research are not as concerned about the subject matter taught to students as much as they are about the values and behaviors acquired during the academic process. Subject matter is part of what is known as formal education, while values and behaviors are part of what is known as informal education. Both of these education types are described below for a better understanding of what they are and what they do.

Formal education

This is the process by which students acquire knowledge via formalized, traditional, and established methods of learning. Examples include (1) specific subjects in the hard sciences (physics, chemistry, microbiology) and soft sciences (social studies, humanities, history), and (2) the grading that takes place based on students' ability to show they have retained that knowledge.

Formal education is typically "fact-based" with the teachings coming from what has already been learned and considered accurate, truthful, and repeatable with the same results. For example, $2 + 2 = 4$ is a math equation that produces the same answer every time it is employed.

Informal education

This is the process by which students learn the behaviors that are expected of them by society. It establishes the values and norms that guide people for the rest of their lives, and it occurs in school and at home. Examples include learning table manners, maintaining personal hygiene, choosing proper clothing for an occasion, and conversing with others.

Informal education also comes from what has already been learned and considered accurate, truthful, and repeatable, but it also stems from what people determine to be appropriate; thereby making it susceptible to change over time. For example, formal white shirts and ties were part of normal attire for many high school students in the 1960s, but this changed to informal blue jeans and T-shirts in the 1970s.

A simple example of an educational study is as follows:

> Angelina is a sociologist researching the adaptation to change for freshmen college students who are away at school and living outside of their family homes for the first time in their lives. Specifically, she wants to measure the impact of college life on their time management skills. She does these using one-on-one interviews and group discussions with the students to determine if living away from home has negatively or positively affected their ability to properly manage the personal and educational aspects of their lives.

The above study examines an educational group of people in a similar situation that they have never experienced before in their lives. Both types of methodologies used to search for similarities are qualitative, but they differ in the ways that they gather information. One-on-one interviews are designed to extract individual thoughts of the students without any type of influence from others to search for patterns of similar thinking. This is beneficial because all responses are internal and specific to the individual without external pressure. Group discussions are designed for students to expand on each other's thinking to find common ground. This is beneficial because students act as sounding boards for each other, so they can find and express ideas that they might not have been able to come up with on their own.

Race

Some scientists argue that there is no real separation of the races since the DNA of all people is very similar. However, for the purposes of this book, race is defined by the differing physical characteristics that people inherit. These characteristics can be seen and typically include skin color, body features (especially facial), hair color, and sometimes eye color.

Please keep in mind that racial differences are limited to physical attributes, and there are no scientific findings that indicate one race is more intelligent than another. Standardized intelligence testing has been conducted in the past, and differences were discovered, but these tests were later determined to be invalid based on the fact that people scored differently based on their environments and experiences. In short, the tests were biased against certain races due to the members' cultural backgrounds.

Racism warrants some discussion in this section because it is a direct result of racial differences. Although it is not always the focus of sociological research, racism exists all over the world, and it has the potential to rear its ugly head during any study involving race. Essentially, racism is a tool used to gain or maintain a power imbalance. It includes any type of prejudice or discriminatory actions (and even thoughts) directed toward a specific race of people.

Racism causes many different problems and can inflict a lot of unnecessary pain on people. Members of targeted groups are "pigeonholed" into categories based on their personal appearances that they cannot escape. Pre-existing thoughts about their behavior, intelligence, and personality exist without any type of justifiable proof or support. They lose job opportunities to those deemed more appropriate for the positions, are banned from certain social groups and settings, and can become withdrawn, angry, depressed, or resentful due to the situations they find themselves in. In some cases, despair leads those being discriminated against to commit acts that reinforce their stereotypes in the minds of their oppressors. For example, members of a group of poor people thought of as thieves might be shunned by employers when looking for jobs, thereby leading them to steal from others in order to survive.

Of greater interest is the fact that the effects of racism can linger long after the reason for its initial occurrence no longer exists. For example, the derogatory acronym "WOP" originated when Italian people immigrated to the United States. Sometimes these individuals did not have the proper documentation to be in the country legally, and "WOP" was short for "without papers."

Race is a unique area for sociological research due to its permanence. People can change many things in their lives, but race is not one of those things. They are born a certain race, and they will die that same race. Unfortunately, stereotypes and prejudices are sometimes associated with specific races, leading to the erroneous lumping of every member into the same category. This generalization has led to heated discussions on race and is a major reason why so much has been written about the topic. It is also a reason why sociologists are attracted to it for research purposes.

Race is also a hot research topic due to the many variables that impact it. Finances, religion, age, politics, social status, and personal experiences all influence people in unique ways; thereby resulting in differing member viewpoints within specific races. These differences can make it challenging for researchers to identify specific patterns that exist for entire races. However, they also indicate the need for understanding all races as the world becomes a global melting pot of human behavior.

A simple example of a racial study is as follows:

> Manuel is a sociologist studying patterns related to race and home purchases in large metropolitan areas. Specifically, he is examining Hispanic home buyer purchases in traditionally white neighborhoods in 12 different metropolitan areas of the United States. He wants to see if these purchases have increased from 2010 to 2019 when compared to the previous decade. He does this mainly using content analysis of documents obtained from the U.S. Census Bureau, but he also interviews local Hispanic leaders for more in-depth insight.

The above study examines home purchases in large metropolitan areas to see if patterns emerge for Hispanic buyers. The content analysis utilizes quantitative methodology to provide concrete numbers that compare Hispanic purchases over specific time periods. The interviews use qualitative methodology to extract information from the Hispanics that might determine influences on their purchasing decisions.

These methods work well in combination due to their different approaches for discovering patterns.

Gender

Anyone who has filled out a questionnaire at a doctor's office is probably familiar with a question asking them to identify their gender or sex. This question is looking for a "male" or "female" answer, but many sociologists do not think the answer is this simple. They view sex and gender as being different terms with distinct meanings. Sex refers to the physical differences between human beings, including reproductive systems, genitalia, strength, and size. Gender refers to traits and behaviors, typically determined by society, traditionally associated with men and women.

Since sex and gender are not considered to be the same, it should not be surprising that a person's sex does not always correlate with that individual's gender. A girl born with female genitalia is identified as female at the beginning of her life. However, as she matures and develops her thoughts, she might start to identify will traditionally male aspects of society. If this happens, she might identify her sex as female and her gender as male. Not surprisingly, many people in the world do not agree with her having the right to identify her gender as male.

The fact that some people believe gender is determined by nature and remains permanent, while others believe that it is determined by the individual and can change over time, makes gender a hot topic of discussion today. However, a debate on how gender is determined needs to be reserved for another discussion. This book views gender, regardless of how it is established, as something that separates the human species into two distinct categories known as male and female.

Sociological research involving gender offers many opportunities since men and women are often part of the same groups. For example, studies involving decision-making in an organization include the following:

- The influence of gender decision-making
- The perception of gender decision-making
- The differences in gender decision-making
- The similarities of gender decision-making
- The success of gender decision-making

The above list is far from complete, but it gives a general idea of the types of gender research that could be conducted and shows the wide-openness for expansion depending on the researcher's particular interest.

A simple example of a gender study is as follows:

> Lori believes gender impacts colon cancer prevention group members' commitment to the cause. She tests her thinking in two ways. First, she measures the relationship between gender and commitment by issuing surveys (with Likert rating scales) to all members. These surveys measure the members' commitment while asking them to designate their gender. The results are then examined for relationships. Second, she directly observes the actions of the members to see if she can establish visible commitment patterns of either

gender. Commitment is shown by the amount of time members spend working to fund colon cancer research, the effort they put forward supporting people who have the disease, and their level of dedication to the goals and objectives of the group.

The above study examines members of a colon cancer prevention group to see if commitment patterns emerge for males or females. The survey is designed to find how members view themselves and their commitment to the cause, with the intent being to discover their beliefs and feelings. The direct observation functions as an external analysis that is designed to be more objective and remove some of the biases that people might have about themselves and their commitment to the cause.

Age

It has been said that "age is only in a person's mind." This might be true in some ways, but the body continues to move forward in time regardless of an individual's thoughts. However, as many people have experienced, maintaining a positive attitude and "thinking young" does wonders for feeling better about the aging process.

One statement that can be made about it is the fact that it is concrete. When a person is a certain age, the laws of nature dictate that it cannot be debated or changed. This is not true for other areas of sociological research interest, such as religion, education, culture...and even gender. For example, people can change their religion or culture simply by moving to a different one, and their education can change by taking new courses. Additionally, gender can change since, as also mentioned earlier, it refers to the traits and behaviors of men and women that are traditionally determined by society...and societies change over time.

Age is an interesting area of study for sociological researchers because, without exception, it has impacted every one of them. They have all aged over time, some more than others, and they know what it is like to progress from one stage of life to another. They also all fall into three main generations that classify them based on age. These generations are the Baby Boomers, Generation X, and Millennials. Each is described below for a better understanding of their existence in society.

Baby Boomers

Baby Boomers (people born early-1940s to mid-1960s) are the generation after the Silent Generation (people born mid-1920s to early-1940s) and before Generation X (people born mid-1960s to the early-1980s). They are often the children of people who fought in World War II, but they are not totally defined by this characteristic because some of their parents have no military background.

One rather interesting fact about Baby Boomers involves money. They were the wealthiest generation born up until that time, and they truly believed that their lifestyles would exceed that of their parents in terms of material comfort. They viewed the world as a place that would continuously improve, and they would reap the benefits of that improvement.

Baby Boomers were the first generation in the United States to not worry about food, shelter, or clothing. These basic necessities were plentiful for most of the Boomers, and programs were in place to help those who truly were in need. Since their needs were met without a struggle, Baby Boomers were sometimes thought of by older generations as being lazy with a sense of entitlement. However, this thinking eroded over time because future generations had even less worry about basic necessities.

In the United States, Baby Boomers will forever be known as the generation that created a spike in birth rates. This increase resulted from post-war families being established. Some people speculate that the larger families were a result of people thinking the World War II victory guaranteed good times in the future. In a sense, the high from being a free country spilled over into the boomer generation and resulted in the confidence that families would be able to take care of themselves.

Another interesting fact about Baby Boomers is their cultural division. Those born early in the generation had a strong association with the Vietnam War, rock music such as The Beatles and the Rolling Stones, and the politics of the late 1960s. However, this identity was not shared by the boomers born late in the generation. These individuals did not view war as a concern, shunned traditional rock and roll for punk and disco, and did not have strong political ties. The extent of this cultural split has been debated, but it was a reality in many instances.

Notable events remembered most by Baby Boomers include the Cuban Missile Crisis, the Cold War, the assassination of the Kennedys and Martin Luther King, the first Super Bowl, the Civil Rights Movement, walking on the moon, the Vietnam War, anti-war protests, the Energy Crisis, the hippy sub-culture, and the Sexual Revolution.

Generation X

Generation X (people born mid-1960s to early-1980s) includes the individuals born after the Baby Boomers (people born early-1940s to mid-1960s) and before the Millennials (people born early-1980s to mid-1990s). They are often the children of older Baby Boomers, meaning their parents might have seen time-fighting in Korea or Vietnam.

This generation was the first to experience two major changes. The first change was an increase in divorces. Their parents no longer felt obligated to remain together, and the number of marital separations reached record levels. The second change was being watched by someone else during the day while their mother and/or father worked. Married parents began to see the economic advantages of both people earning income, and single parents had to work to support their families. In a sense, Generation X kids were the first to see traditional values decrease in importance as society put adults' wants ahead of children's needs.

Hip-hop, grunge, and rap were big musical influences on Generation X youth. Kurt Cobain was seen as a symbol of this generation, and, except for traditional blues that were the roots of rock and roll, white people began to stray into the music of black culture.

Unfortunately, Generation X was the first to experience the dreaded AIDS virus, and over one million people were HIV positive. At the time, there was no effective treatment or remedy, and many people died. The only way to fight the future spread of this tragic disease was to educate people on how to prevent it, so sex education made it into every school, regardless of the conservative thinking of the administration. It appeared that the free love movement that started with hippies in the 1960s had severe consequences and needed to come to an end.

Notable events remembered most by Generation X individuals include the tearing down of the Berlin Wall, the introduction of MTV, the indie film movement, the first computerized games, Prince Charles and Lady Diana's royal wedding, the Challenger shuttle disaster, and the first Gulf War.

Millennials

Millennials (people born early-1980s to mid-1990s) are the generation after Generation X (people born mid-

1960s to the early-1980s) and before Generation Z (people born mid-1990s to mid-2000s). They are often children of the Baby Boomers (born mid-1940s to early-1960s) and are sometimes referred to as "Echo Boomers."

Unlike the Baby Boomers, Millennials are not geared toward having large families. Some people suggest that the smaller family mentality stems from the "me generation" and self-centeredness that these people have associated with them. This suggestion might or might not be true, but the Millennials' narcissistic ideology serves a useful purpose because it instills the confidence necessary to stand up for the things they believe in and value.

Millennials are the first generation to be born into computer technology; thereby finding it easier than previous generations to make adjustments to new technological advances. This generation also tends to take a liberal stand on political issues...especially those involving the environment and religion.

Millennials were greatly impacted by the economic recession that occurred from the late 2000s to early 2010s because they found themselves unemployed, with little hope of finding high-paying jobs. This was reflected in Millennials believing that wealth is paramount. However, their outlook changed as they gradually moved into management positions in organizations.

Notable events remembered most by Millennials include 9/11, digital music, digital books, online businesses, record stock market numbers, political correctness, viral videos, blogging, minority protests, police brutality, and the first black president.

Sociologists sometimes conduct research involving age using generations as boundaries for the people they are studying. Essentially, these generations are the groups that contain the members used as participants in the studies. A simple example is as follows:

Claudia is a sociologist researching baby boomers and marijuana. Specifically, she wants to see if people in this generation support legalizing this drug for recreational use, and she does this with surveys and one-on-one interviews. She sends out a survey to all members in the Greater Chicago (Illinois) Chapter of the American Association of Retired Persons (AARP). The survey asks the age of the participant (to determine baby boomer status) and if they support the legalization of marijuana for medical or recreational use. She also randomly selects 50 people from a list of the AARP Chicago Chapter baby boomer members and interviews them one-on-one via telephone.

The above study examines retired baby boomers from a select group within the American Association of Retired Persons (AARP) to see if they support the legalization of marijuana for recreational purposes. The survey is quantitatively designed to identify baby boomers within the Chicago AARP chapter and ask them their opinion on the subject matter. The interviews qualitatively gather information that might show why individual boomers feel the way they do about marijuana use. These methods work well in combination due to their different methodological approaches to discovering patterns.

Sexual orientation

There is often debate about how sexual orientation is defined. However, for the purposes of this book, it is defined as "a person's sexual orientation refers to the gender to which he or she is attracted." It involves an individual's pattern of attraction to the same gender, another gender, or both genders and is divided into the following categories:

Opposite gender (heterosexual)

This sexual orientation is considered by many people to be the most acceptable category because males are attracted to females and females are attracted to males. Traditional families were built on a male (father) and female (mother) relationship where each played a different role in working, running the household, and raising children.

Same gender (homosexual)

This sexual orientation occurs when males are attracted to males or females are attracted to females. It is not as traditionally accepted as the opposite gender (heterosexual), but it is gaining popularity within mainstream societies. Quite simply, homosexual individuals are more open now about their sexuality than they have ever been in the past because non-homosexuals are able to accept and embrace the idea that people are different.

Both genders (bisexual)

People who are attracted to both males and females fall into this category. In short, this means that men and women are attracted to men and women. However, contrary to what some people believe, this does not always mean there is an equal attraction to both genders. People might prefer one gender over another, but they are open to sexual relationships with either, so they classify themselves as bisexual.

No gender (asexual)

People who are not attracted to either gender fall into this category. These individuals might still engage in sexual activities, but they engage for different reasons, including the wish to please their partners or the desire to have children. Interestingly, asexual individuals have been known to be discriminated against by certain members of the LGBTQ+ (lesbian, gay, bisexual, transgender) community because some LGBTQ+s assume that anyone who is not homosexual or bisexual must be straight...which is not true for asexual people.

Sociologists who have research interests in sexual orientation have more opportunities today than they have ever had in the past simply because the public is more aware and accepting of different sexual preferences than ever before. LBGT awareness campaigns, reality TV shows, and the willingness of those with different sexual orientations to "come out of the closet" have changed public perception. In terms of sexual preferences, the mainstream has been diluted, and so have acceptable norms.

A simple example of a sexual orientation study is as follows:

> Darnell wants to study male homosexual military veterans to see if they experience types of discrimination not experienced by homosexuals who were never affiliated with the military. To do this, he sends surveys to all members of the LGBTQ+ Detroit (Michigan) headquarters. These surveys ask for the members' gender, sexual orientation, and military experience, along with a detailed account of their discriminatory experiences. Additionally, Darnell meets separately with three groups of male homosexual military veterans and three groups of male homosexuals with no military experience. These groups are all made up of members from the LGBT Detroit headquarters, and the discussions focus on the specific types of discrimination that these individuals have experienced.

The above study compares male homosexual members of the LGBT Detroit chapter who are war veterans to those who have no military experience. The research is designed to see if military veterans experience discrimination patterns that are not experienced by those who have never been in the military. The survey gets the respondents to describe the discrimination that they have experienced without input from others. The

Group discussions are designed for men to expand on each other's thoughts to discover common discriminatory factors. The group setting is beneficial because the men act as sounding boards for each other, so they can discuss factors that they might not have thought of on their own. These methods work well together because the survey uses quantitative methodology while the group discussions are more qualitative in design.

Health

Sociologists typically believe that health is comprised of physical, mental, and emotional factors. Their research often involves exploring the way social factors impact the health of individuals and groups within society. For example, they might look at the influence poverty has on the movement of AIDS from one person to another.

The most important health discoveries made by sociologists involve the spread of disease. Their research has shown that disease spreads from factors that are not related to nature or biology. For example, urbanization and globalization often play a role, as do culture, beliefs, and traditions. Medical researchers do an excellent job of gathering information on diseases, but they often fail to address the societal reasons for their occurrence in specific demographics...which is precisely why the work of sociologists is valuable.

One of the most interesting sociological findings regarding the spread of disease involves its relationship to socio-economic status. This variable is described below for a better understanding of what it involves and why it is important.

Socioeconomic status

Essentially, socioeconomic status refers to the social standing of people, groups, or communities. Contrary to what some people think, it is not a fancy term for income because it involves two other factors. These factors are job status and education, and, in combination, all three have a positive or negative impact on the quality of people's lives.

Income refers to the amount of money that people earn. It also includes net worth because investments, savings, and tangible assets are also taken into account. Income has a direct impact on people's ability to buy things and provide for themselves and their families.

Education refers to the level of education that people have achieved. Higher education often leads to better job opportunities, and higher education also requires higher income to obtain. So, the impact here is somewhat circular because higher earnings lead to better educational opportunities, which lead to higher income potential.

Job status, also known as occupation, refers to the positions people hold to earn income. This factor is more difficult to assess in terms of impact when compared to income and education because it is somewhat subjective. For example, a plumber and an attorney might earn the same yearly wage, but people's opinions differ over the value and importance of each job; thereby resulting in differences in the impact this has on socio-economic status. However, it can be said that high-paying professions typically require higher skill levels and more education when compared to jobs that pay less money.

One thing that should be noted about socioeconomic status is that it is used for more than just academic research. It is usually discussed in terms of social science, but organizations and governmental agencies at all levels gather data related to it and make determinations based on the interpretation of that data.   For example, people are often classified as low, middle, and high socioeconomic status based on government analyses.

Socioeconomic status can have a profound impact on people, groups, and communities. For example, people with low socioeconomic status have been shown to have high rates of physical health issues such as obesity and diabetes. Those same individuals also report higher than normal cases of mental health issues, including depression and drug abuse. In terms of communities, those with low socioeconomic status are often impacted by higher rates of poverty, crime, and unemployment. Unfortunately, communities with high minority and elderly populations often feel the negative impact of low socioeconomic status more directly than communities with less diversity.

A simple example of a study involving socioeconomic status is as follows:

Juanita is a sociologist conducting research on the impact of low socioeconomic status on infant mortality rates of babies born to urban Baltimore (Maryland) teenage mothers, as compared to the rest of the nation. She does so through content analysis of data provided by the US Census and the Baltimore Public School System. Specifically, she uses the data to compare infant mortality rates of low socioeconomic status teenage mothers nationally to those of low socioeconomic status teenage mothers in Baltimore schools.

The above study examines a select demographic of low socioeconomic teenage mothers to see how their babies' infant mortality rates compare to those of teenage mothers in the same situation nationally. The content analysis uses quantitative methodology to provide concrete numbers that show infant mortality for each group in the study. The numbers are then compared to see if statistical differences emerge between the two groups.

Gangs

Gangs are an interesting area for research due to the fact that negativity is often associated with them. Robbery, drugs, and violence are three unpleasant happenings that come to mind when people think about gangs, but the list gets even more cynical when these groups of individuals are tied to things such as extortion, human trafficking, kidnapping, and prostitution.

Large gangs with defined chains of command and structured hierarchies, such as mafia families and drug cartels, have been known to oversee empires larger than some Fortune 500 companies...with a profit margin that those companies can only dream about. In fact, at a certain point in their existence, one particular drug cartel in Mexico was said to have had more money at their disposal than the Mexican Government.

A gang, however, does not need to be big and organized in order to have influence. Smaller, local gangs often have a major cultural impact on their communities in terms of music, clothing, shoes, and even team sports affiliations. Sometimes that impact moves past the local communities and into the mainstream, thereby resulting in changes on a much larger scale. However, regardless of the geographical boundaries, the influence of gangs makes researching them attractive to sociologists and other social scientists.

One thing about gangs that deserves mention is that the internal actions of members are sometimes wrongly perceived. This is because gangs, like many other groups in society, are often unfairly stereotyped by those who do not understand them. For example, membership is not always fixed. The "once a member, always a member" mentality does not always exist, and people are not necessarily "beat in, and beat out" when entering or leaving the gang. Some members get into gangs when they are young, but eventually drift away as their interests and concerns about life change without any type of violence.

A simple example of a sociological study involving gangs is as follows:

> Manfred is a sociologist researching a well-known and locally feared street gang in Albuquerque (New Mexico). He wants to see if the gang is an organized group with a

highly structured hierarchy or a less coherent group with limited hierarchical structure. To do this, he hangs out with various gang members and observes their activities. He also conducts one-on-one interviews with some of the gang members to gain an understanding of how they view the gang's purpose, its leadership, and the behavior of its members.

The above study examines a gang to gain insight into its organization and hierarchical structure. The one-on-one interviews expose the individual thoughts of members to see how they feel about the gang's purpose and leadership, and the direct observation removes some of the bias that the gang members might have about the activities within. When combined, these two qualitative processes provide a useful methodology for gathering data and discovering patterns.

Crime

Many people are infatuated with the crime that occurs in society. They read books, watch films, and listen to podcasts that deal with crime...especially the cases that involve murder and/or mystery. One reason for these individuals' infatuation is their desire to figure out why criminals do what they do from a psychological perspective. Other reasons for the attraction to crime include people's interest in analyzing the fairness of trials, judging the decisions of juries, and forming opinions on the sentencing of those found guilty. Quite simply, criminals live their lives in ways that many people are not comfortable with or familiar with, so they follow crime stories in an attempt to get a better understanding.

Sociologists interested in research involving crime examine the behavior of people who break laws. These laws are established group, cultural, and societal norms that are upheld and enforced by designated authorities. Authorities also organize trials and punish those who have been found to deviate from or violate the norms.

Crime studies can be one of the most difficult types of research for sociologists because, as cultures change, so do the criminal laws within...and those law changes can alter the perception of what is considered to be deviant behavior. For example, it is now legal in many societies to use marijuana even though some members still perceive it to be wrong. This perception makes it difficult for researchers to gather interview information because some people view laws as being broken even though they no longer exist. Along the same lines, crime statistics are skewed when searching for law-breaking patterns because those patterns are irrelevant based on the fact that the applicable laws no longer exist. This might seem a bit confusing, but the main point here is that everyone in society does not view laws the same...especially when those laws change, and people's values and beliefs are compromised.

A simple example of a sociological study involving crime is as follows:

> Bertram is a sociologist who is examining serial killers to discover patterns that help explain why they kill people and lead to ideas for future preventative measures. To do this, he travels to prisons and conducts one-on-one interviews with convicted serial killers. Before the interviews, he reads all of the information he can find

about their crimes, including their case files from the police, so he can tailor each interview to the specific killer.

The above study examines serial killers to gain insight into the reasons for their crimes and help find ways to prevent this type of behavior in others. The one-on-one interviews tap into the minds of the killers to see if patterns for their actions exist. The content analysis informs the researcher about the specifics of each case and prepares him for the individual interviews. These two qualitative methodologies work together to discover information that can be used to prevent similar killings in the future.

Immigration

Immigration is a topic that interests the government of just about every nation in the world because, in one way or another, they are impacted by it. Some countries try to stop people from leaving their borders, while others limit the number of people that come in, but the fact remains that people always have and always will want to move from one country to another.

Sociological studies in immigration often involve factors such as ethnicity, race, government, and politics. This is because people often leave their current homes based on turmoil, stress, or fear resulting from these factors. For example, discriminatory practices, which can be as severe as ethnic cleansing and genocide, often result from political changes that shift the balance of power. New regimes push their own agendas, and some of those agendas place blame for all existing problems on those who are different or minority in status.

Sociological research involving immigration often explores important aspects of existence for members of an immigrant community. Culture, religion, education, language barriers, social status, and financial well-being are examples of those aspects. A simple example of a sociological study involving immigration is as follows:

> Nadia is a sociologist researching the ways in which an urban neighborhood in Cleveland (Ohio) provides for and serves the cultural needs of Chaldean immigrants moving into the community. She does this by conducting group interviews where she asks the Chaldean member to discuss their culture and the needs associated with it. She also conducts a content analysis of community information to find documentation of practices that address the cultural needs of Chaldeans. Last, but certainly not least, she directly observes the Chaldean immigrants regarding their actions and activities within the community.

The above study examines the ways in which the cultural needs of immigrating Chaldeans are served. The group interviews tap into the thoughts of members of the Chaldean community to define their cultural needs, the content analysis provides statistical data on what is currently being done in the community in terms of servicing the needs of the immigrants, and the direct observation eliminates some of the bias that might be associated with the group interviews. In combination, these methods allow the research to be conducted from a quantitative and qualitative perspective.

48

Part Three

Ethical concerns

It should not come as a surprise that sociological research has the potential to create ethical concerns. If conducted properly, there is little concern here, but, unfortunately, not everyone puts forth the time and effort to make sure their research is proper. When ethical principles are violated, there is sure to be some type of fallout.

Not surprisingly, the fallout from ethical violations can be serious. Examples include studies involving the health of human subjects. People who are subjected to medical studies might suffer irreversible damage to their minds or bodies that result in them suffering adverse effects for the rest of their lives. One only needs to look at the concentration camp "medical" studies conducted by the Nazi Regime in World War II to see how ethical violations can result in death and destruction of human lives.

It can be argued that the medical studies conducted by the Germans were far beyond ethical violations and would be considered immoral and illegal by any government other than the Third Reich, so this might not be the best example. However, the United States has also conducted its fair share of unethical studies where human health was jeopardized. An example of one of these studies is shown below.

LSD Studies

In the early 1950s, the Central Intelligence Agency (CIA) decided to conduct experiments on humans using the psychedelic drug Lysergic Acid Diethylamide (LSD). It was part of a top-secret CIA project codenamed MK-Ultra that was designed to see if people's behavior could be modified using LSD for mind control.

At first, the subjects of this study were willing participants. However, that changed as the CIA began to think about using LSD as a truth serum or a form of psychological weapon on the minds of enemy leaders. At the time, this seemed to make sense because the United States was in the midst of a cold war with communist nations, and non-military intellectual battles needed to be fought and won on the metaphorical front lines. It also seemed sensible to start using subjects without their consent to see how they would react after being completely unaware of what was happening to them. At this point, the study became dubious in nature with serious ethical concerns.

Research was conducted on United States and Canadian citizens in hospitals, prisons, and universities. Sometimes the leaders of these institutions were informed of what was happening to the people in their organizations, but other times they were left in the dark.

A United States project that drew harsh criticism for using subjects without their consent was known as "Operation Midnight Climax." This project involved brothels in San Francisco, California. Prostitutes were sent out on the streets to lure victims back to the brothels for sex, but they were instead given LSD, and their actions were monitored by CIA personnel hiding behind one-way glass. Everything about this project was illegal, and some people felt the negative effects for the rest of their lives.

A particularly horrendous Canadian study fell under the jurisdiction of British psychiatrist Donald Evan Cameron. Dr. Cameron placed some of his subjects into drug-induced comas for several weeks at a time while continuously playing tape loops of repetitive statements, music, or noise.   Some of his subjects were negatively impacted for the rest of their lives, with loss of memory being one of the biggest problems.

The adverse reactions suffered by people after unknowingly consuming LSD were plentiful, and death resulted in some cases. The most notable death was Frank Olsen, a biochemist in the US Army, who, according to CIA records, jumped to his death from the 13th floor of a building in New York City. Olsen's family, however, never accepted the story about him committing suicide. They believe that he was murdered because he was a government security risk based on what he knew about highly classified CIA programs. Their beliefs were later substantiated when Olsen's body was exhumed several years after his death. It was found by a medical examiner that he was knocked unconscious before exiting the window, thereby indicating suspicion of foul play and potential murder.

The MK-Ultra project lasted about 20 years, and it was not until the end that information about the research conducted began to reach the public. When people found out what happened, some were shocked and left wondering why the United States government would allow such a study to progress. People demanded more information about MK-Ultra, but when efforts were made to collect more details, it was found that much of the documentation had been destroyed by the CIA.

Fortunately, today's sociological research has little chance of causing serious illness or injury, and death is almost certain not to happen unless something goes drastically wrong. However, some harm can result if ethical standards are not put in place and followed, and this is why the American Sociological Association (ASA) has a code of ethics that sociologists must adhere to when conducting research. This code includes the following:

- Informed consent must be received from all participants in the study.
- Risks and responsibilities of the research must be conveyed to all participants in the study.
- Privacy of all participants in the study must be protected, and confidential information cannot be released.
- All financial support for the research must be disclosed, and there can be no conflicts of interest.
- All researchers must remain unbiased and impartial in regard to the study and its findings.

The above guidelines might seem fairly easy to follow due to the fact that most sociologists want to conduct research that helps people and the societies in which they reside. However, confidentiality can become a major issue if government authorities, such as the police or FBI, want information that they believe can be used to solve crimes, convict criminals, or prove someone's innocence.

In a nutshell, ethical concerns are very important for sociological studies, and the researchers must take responsibility for the work they conduct. They must uncompromisingly (1) guarantee the health and safety of all participants, (2) make sure those participants are fully informed before they consent to participate, and (3) act without bias when conducting research and analyzing results.

Summary

This book provides basic knowledge about the scientific study of society, known more commonly as sociology. It is an excellent resource for beginners or those seeking general knowledge because it explains the basics of the subject matter using simple terminology and easy-to-understand examples. It is also written for easy reader understanding at all levels, and real-world application is a major part of the learning process.

The book is divided into three parts. Part one introduces the concept of sociology, explores micro-sociologist and macro-sociologist types, and explains the differences between quantitative and qualitative methodologies used in research. Part two focuses on specific areas of interest for sociological research, including cults, family, religion, education, race, gender, age, sexual orientation, health, gangs, crime, and immigration.   Part three discusses ethical concerns and summarizes the book as a whole.

Congratulations! You now understand more about sociology...the scientific study of people in societies all over the world.

9 781704 717326